Electric Arches

"Reading Eve L. Ewing's *Electric Arches* is such an awakening and active experience—this book time travels. . . . 'Recall this,' writes Ewing in 'Shea Butter Manifesto,' both as invitation and as spellbinding command. I'm awestruck by the rigor and intimacy of this book, by its insistent love for both black past and black future. Ewing leaves no unnamed ritual uncovered, no implicit idiom uncelebrated. This book is a gift, a visual and lyrical offering to be treasured as gospel."

—Morgan Parker, author of *There Are More Beautiful Things Than Beyoncé*

"Of course she had me at Koko Taylor. She had me again at shea butter and Ron Artest and especially at an eerily intriguing fur suit. This is an effusive celebration of black girlhood in all its muted but relentless sparkle, a tenacious exploration of all its lives, the wide-aloud witnessing of a born storyteller slicing her two-wheeler through the streets of a broken and boisterous city. You won't believe this is Eve Ewing's first book. It's that assured, that crafted. Ever heard Koko Taylor's guttural growl, the lyric that floors you like a backhand slap? It's that too."

—Patricia Smith, author of *Incendiary Art*

"I didn't think it was possible for one book to contain work and worlds that would be loved by eight-year-olds and eighty-year-olds, junior-high-school dropouts and emeritus English professors. I didn't think it was possible for one book to contain the emotional sweat of Chicago, Dorchester, and Yazoo City, Mississippi. I didn't think it was possible for one book to make us smell the residue of classroom erasers, empty White Castle bags and wet wondrous balls of Black girl hair clinging to the bottoms of bathtubs. With *Electric Arches*, Eve Ewing has written a book I thought was un-write-able. The book is as precise as it is ambitious, pulling equally on shared memories and individual imagination. Every page feels like a beginning and end, an invitation and conclusion, but never in that order. Somehow Eve Ewing created a book that is at once formally spectacular and grounded enough to ask readers the two most important questions in art: *will you stop to remember with me?* and *Will you help me change the world with that memory? Electric Arches* is alive."

—Kiese Laymon, author of *Long Division*

"Again and again reading Eve Ewing's *Electric Arches* I felt some blooming in my body, or some flock of herons batting into the air in my body, which I think was indicating something like joy at witnessing the imagination at work in these poems, the imagination born of rigorous attention coupled with critical love. Thankfully, there's a word for all that: tenderness. And the joy is that we learn tenderness by witnessing it. Which is to say, and it's not too much to say, this book is one of the maps to our survival."

—Ross Gay, author of *Catalog of Unabashed Gratitude*

Electric Arches

Eve L. Ewing

Haymarket Books
Chicago, Illinois

to Leila

and

to all the fire city children

Published in 2017 by
Haymarket Books
P.O. Box 180165
Chicago, IL 60618
773-583-7884
www.haymarketbooks.org
info@haymarketbooks.org

ISBN: 978-1-60846-856-0

Trade distribution:
In the US, Consortium Book Sales and Distribution, www.cbsd.com
In Canada, Publishers Group Canada, www.pgcbooks.ca
In the UK, Turnaround Publisher Services, www.turnaround-uk.com
All other countries, Ingram Publisher Services International, IPS_intlsales@ingram.com

This book was published with the generous support of Lannan Foundation and Wallace Action Fund.

Printed in Canada by union labor.

Cover design by Brett Neimann. Cover artwork, *Garden of Lost Things*, by Brianna McCarthy.

Interior artwork by Eve L. Ewing. *Artifacts*, appearing on pages 10–11, photographed by Iván Arenas.

Library of Congress Cataloging-in-Publication data is available.

10 9 8 7 6 5 4 3 2

Contents

foreword

I knew I was thoroughly caught by Eve Ewing's debut collection when I found myself crying—but my spirit also laughing—after I read "the first time [a re-telling]" and ended up sharing stories with my husband about our first, or worst, times facing racism from strangers. Ewing's work reminds me of the reasons I began writing myself, in search of expression or escape that could dull the sharp edges of my life. I, too, have ridden a flying bicycle.

Poets fill in the spaces other types of storytelling can't always reach—childhood memories, the pain of racism, a definitive sense of place and loss. Ewing's work is honest, evocative, surprising, and somehow all the more real for its escapes into the magical. These pieces shine with urgency, truth, and powerful vestiges of childhood. The black speculative arts—science fiction, fantasy, horror, magical realism—are gaining more notice for their ability to show us what's actually real, what matters in the *now*, and Ewing's work falls nicely within a growing community of writers who are leading us through future dreams and glimpses of magic.

Electric Arches is a web we are happy to be caught up in. This collection is delightful.

—Tananarive Due

A note of introduction

When I was a little girl, I was allowed to ride my bicycle from one end of the block to the other, because that way my mother could come outside and stand on the sidewalk and see me. Chicago is very flat, so when you stand outside and look down the street you can pretty much see to the end of the planet. Anyway, as I rode my bike I would narrate, in my head, all of my adventures. In my head I was shooting arrows, exploring dungeons, solving mysteries. In this way, my block became the backdrop of infinite possibility, even if the reality of the cracked cement and the brick wall facing our window and the gangs seemed to constrain that possibility. The space in my head was as real to me as the dirt beneath my feet.

This book is about my life and maybe also your life. And it is about the places we invent. Every story in it is absolutely true. Some of the stories are from the past and some are from the future. In the future, every child in Chicago has food and a safe place to sleep, and mothers laugh all day and eat Popsicles. Every Fourth of July there are big fireworks and no one shoots a gun, not even police because there are no police, and when you go downtown and look up at the sky, the electric arches stretch so far toward heaven that you feel like you might be the smallest and most important thing ever to be born.

Thanks for reading. I appreciate you.

e.e.

true stories

SENSATIONAL! STARTLING! NEW!

WHAT ARE THEY SAYING?

Arrival Day

Black revolutionaries do not drop from the moon. We are created by our conditions.
—Assata Shakur

it happened under cover of night or early morning
depending on who you ask. the hour when the press
stops running. when the baker arrives and unlocks
the door. the cables came down, silent and charcoal,
matte and slithering. they hit the earth and coiled at
the foot of a tree, on a bus-stop bench, atop a mound
of cigarette butts in front of the dialysis center. later
when the NASA boys looked for footage of the arrival
—surely some security camera in some parking lot,
somewhere in America...?—that hour was all
blank, everywhere, all blank, like as if each of them
had a magnet for a beating heart, their veins murmuring
clear it away, clear it away, until the tape was empty.

in the years before, when hateful men warned of the coming,
crushing aluminum cans in their hands while their
friends threw darts, or in rowboats tying flies, they
spoke only of darkness. 'their eyes will be dirt,' the men said,
'and they will cover the windows with tar in the places where we
talk to god. they will seize our daughters who
will return to us in rags, holding mud babies and
asking for a room to sleep.' the hateful men and their
wives wore reading glasses and drank cinnamon tea
on the days when they wrote letters to each other about

how the coming people would steal, how they loved
the sound of grinding teeth in place of real music,
how the girl ones were greedy and lustful and
felt no pain but made endless noise and how small ones could
trick you, looking like children, but their skin was mercury
and they could not be shot dead so do not fall for it.
they wrote their letters on glass and plastic and metal.
they said 'they are coming and they will paint everything black.'

so they had no words for the moon people when they did come.
and the moon people could not be captured. camera lenses
looking on them turned to salt and cast white trails across the
eyelids of the looker. and the moon people were dressed in
every color. they wore saffron yellow and Kool cigarette green and
Georgia clay red and they wore violet, they wore violet. and they
were loud. as their hands worked, hammering the iron of the
jail cell doors into lovely wrought curls and bicycle chains,
smashing the fare boxes at the train stations into wind chimes
and bowing low to the passengers as they entered—some sashaying
through the turnstile, some dropping it low as they went underneath,
they sang. the moon people had been listening all this time and
they knew all about Sam Cooke and Aretha Franklin and Mahalia
Jackson and Marvin Gaye and Missy Elliott, and they sang while
they smashed a bottle on the squad cars—a Hennessy bottle or
a Coke or a pressed kale juice, whatever was near enough to say 'this
here is christened a new thing.' and they drove them down my street
and your street and your street, the tires painted to look like vinyl 45s
and the children tied yarn and ribbons to the windshield wipers
and the moon people turned them on high so that as they drove, the colors
waved in the sunlight, which was now streaming so clearly

onto the porch where i sat rubbing the rusting chain of the swing and thinking
of grass when the boy down the street, who in smaller days I walked
to school when his mother worked early, who loved lime
popsicles the best, who danced his way from his own porch to the basketball
court in the afternoon, who the police had recently declared a man, stopping
him mid-two-step to ask questions he could not answer because the query beneath
them was 'why are you alive' and none of us can say, the boy, he came to me and walked
up the steps where the paint is peeling and knelt at my side, and i did not
look him in the eye. instead i watched a firefly, the first of the summer, land on his left
shoulder, and i thought 'here are two glowing ones,' but he did not notice,
only held my hand and told me 'we are free now.' and i could not
believe i had lived to see it—the promised light, descended to us at last.

the first time [a re-telling]

I was six years old. I know I must have been six because I was on a two-wheeler bike by myself and my dad gave it to me for my sixth birthday. We lived on Fletcher. I was riding the bike up and down the block. I was allowed to go from one corner to the other by myself because that way my mom or anyone could see me if they just looked for me. The old white lady came down the block from time to time and sometimes she was nice and sometimes she was mean. She had short brown hair and small eyes. She always wore a heavy coat. This time she screamed at me. "You little nigger! You almost hit me with that bike! Go back to your nigger Jesse Jackson neighborhood!" I told my mom and she told me the flying bike should only be for weekends, but okay, I could use it just this once. I ran back out and the lady was still there. I flew up on my bike and started going around her in small, tight circles until she got very dizzy trying to watch me. Just as she was falling over I scooped her up with my giant net and flew her to the lake. I was going to drop her in the water but I felt bad so I left her on a rock and went home and had a paleta.

The Device

It wasn't like a George Washington Carver kind of thing where one brilliant Negro with a soldering iron made some magic and poof! a miraculous machine. It was an open-source kind of situation. Thousands of high-school science-fair whiz kids, this and that engineering club at this and that technical college, the One Black Person at a bunch of Silicon Valley startups getting together with a bunch of other One Black Persons over craft beer and coding late into the night, even some government folks working off the clock (or so the rumors go). Not just one person. A hive mind of Black nerds, obsessive types, scientists and inventors but also historians and archaeologists and the odd astrologer here and there. Project Delta Mother, they called it (goofy name tbh but it's whatever).

When the time came to flip the switch, the sentimental poetic ones who were in charge of communication and media and symbolism got the idea that it should be the youngest among them to do it. She stood at the front of the stage and seemed unfazed by how long the speeches went on, everyone wanting a moment at the podium to give a benediction or remember a lost comrade or shed a tear or play a short video that never turned out to be that short. She was a gangly one, a fifth grader from Providence who had started showing up at the high-school robotics team meetings when the afterschool science enrichment course at her own school got cut. Her grandmother had bought her a special dress for this momentous occasion, and she didn't want to wear it but didn't want to hurt Gramma's feelings either, so as the starched frill rubbed against the backs of her legs and made her itchy she tried to distract herself by counting the tiles on the ceiling. She was so engrossed and the speeches were so many that she almost didn't hear her name when it was called. The man in the lab coat whose name she had forgotten beckoned her toward the device, as the au-

dience stood reverent and waiting. Their arms were all in the air to take photos and videos, and she thought they looked like they were about to go down a waterslide, and that made her smile, which made them smile.

DILIGENT

SEEKING

She stood before the machine. It hummed at a low resonance, making her teeth feel funny as she got closer to it. Its ten thousand tiny lights popped into and out of momentary existence every few seconds, twinkling bravely though the theater was bright inside. She blinked at it, and began quietly humming to herself.

The man in the lab coat watched her watching the device. After so many late nights with this hulking thing, seeing it in the light of day made him click his tongue. This day was no sleek reveal. No one would be gasping over pocket sizing and carefully beta-tested user interfaces. The device was an inelegant hodgepodge, a reflection of the hands that made it. Bits and pieces stuck out of crevices where they should have been hidden— wire, shards of hastily sawn PVC, the odd patch of duct tape. It looked like in a hundred years it might be something you'd find at a yard sale. But of course, he thought after a second, wouldn't that be a success? Shouldn't the device come to be so average and commonplace that it ceases to be magic and comes to be part of everyday life for regular black people all over the country? Wasn't that the dream? He tilted his head slightly as though it might show him a new angle on the whole thing—just as the girl reached out for the switch.

In that split second, he realized for the first time that the machine might be dangerous. That having a child be the one to do it was symbolic, sure, and also very, very stupid. This was the thought that entered his head as the room filled with flashing lights, and he began to panic. The device was going to explode and kill them all, and the girl would be first to die, and he would live just long enough to see it happen.

But no. Those were flashbulbs. And a thousand journalists, official and not-so-much, captured the moment when the girl activated the device. It roared to life, its internal cooling fans whirring furiously, lights blinking faster and faster. People in the audience began to cry. One man, a pastor who had led a booming rendition of "Lift Every Voice," fainted. The girl stayed very calm. She had read the manual many times.

"Hello," she said. Her voice cracked, and she cleared her dry throat and repeated herself, loudly this time. "Hello!" Everyone else in the room fell silent. They waited.

The device's external speakers began to crackle, like a phone sounds when wind is blowing over the mouthpiece. And then the reply came back, loud and clear. Almost too loud. The man in the lab coat covered his ears. "Hello? Who—Lord, I have prayed for this day! I knew you would find favor with me as you have with my sister Willa. If you only guide my steps, I will be faithful."

The man in the lab coat looked, wild-eyed, at the girl. He began to gesture at her frantically, but she only nodded, unperturbed, and pulled a folded-up piece of paper out of her dress pocket. She had practiced for this. As the audience looked on in awe, she spoke, slowly and deliberately. Mostly she had it memorized, but she looked down at the paper every few seconds to be sure not to mess up.

"Hello. Please stay calm. This is not God, or a dream, and you are not going crazy. I am talking to you from many years in the future." She gulped once and continued. "I am using a device built by the colored people of this country." She felt funny saying *colored*, but the history people said it would be better that way. "As you know, we were stolen from our homeland and brought here. We have had many difficulties and our families have been hurt and separated. In my time, we are not slaves. But we face challenges. We need help from our ancestors, but you have been lost to us. So we worked very hard and made this special machine. It allows us to talk to you inside your head, even though we are far apart. It is like yelling over a river." The poets had added that part and it hadn't made much sense when she first practiced that line, but now it seemed right. "I am your great-great-great-granddaughter. I am the first person in history to use this device. People from all over are here with me, watching. We have many questions for you. And other people will use the device to talk to their ancestors, too. So now, Grandmother, my first question is..."

She looked down at the paper to get it exactly right.

"What words can you offer us to help us be free as black people in a world that does not love us?"

The girl stared at the device as though a face might appear amidst the plastic and metal, then gulped again and folded the paper back up and stuck it in a sweaty rectangle back into her pocket. She turned toward the audience, seeing them as though for the first time. The device was crackling and humming and buzzing and shaking and so were they. People had their shoes off and feet up on the seats of the auditorium, rocking forward and back like babies. They wept. They grinned. They scribbled into notebooks and clicked photograph after photograph. They bit their nails. They grasped at each other's shoulders, holding each other up while they waited. And waited. The man in the lab coat sat cross-legged on the stage, leaning against the podium as though alone in his own living room, and stared at her with his mouth agape. She turned back toward the device, wondering if the connection had been lost.

"Grandmoth—" she began. But sound from the device cut her off, echoing across the auditorium, bouncing against brick and plaster and ricocheting in everyone's ears. It was laughter. It began hoarse and raspy and then unfolded into ringing peals and gasps, sounding and resounding louder and louder. The device sputtered and flashed and began to get hot, tape curling off and the smell of melting plastic curling forth from the rear vents, and the audience gasped, and the woman somewhere in America, sometime in America, laughed and laughed and laughed. And the little girl put her hands on her own cheeks and felt their warmth, and the woman laughed. And the lights in the auditorium began to flicker and fade, and still the woman laughed. She laughed, and laughed, and laughed.

four boys on Ellis [a re-telling]

As I was getting into my car I saw the lights flashing and the four of them sitting on the curb. CPD stood over them and the university police were looking on. I drove up and pulled alongside and asked what was going on, if their parents had been called and informed that they were being questioned. Their heads were down. One officer told me that the youngest was nine years old. He said they were suspected of stealing a phone. I asked if they were being arrested or if it was legal protocol to interrogate them without an adult present. Another officer began to yell at me, standing next to my car and shouting through my window. He told me to leave. I would not.

I put the car in park and closed my eyes. I concentrated very hard, picturing the boys at home, eating cereal and watching Naruto. When I opened them, the police were shouting and jumping into the air, grasping at the boys' shoelaces as they drifted upward into the clear night. Their bikes went up, too, and they managed to climb atop them midair, which was impressive. They seemed to have forgotten the police and didn't notice me, only looking at each other and smiling and singing as they flew.

Sestina with Matthew Henson's Fur Suit

I was reading poems in a small town far from home,
in a museum of taxidermy and curiosities:
a coyote, a plaster replica of Winged Victory.
The air conditioner turned my hands to ice.
Safia was there, and Hanif, and Jayson, dressed in black.
I was grateful they guarded me from lonely.

All the people in the town seemed a little lonely.
The children spoke only of fleeing home.
They sang sad songs and painted their nails black
and asked us everything, indulging their curiosities
while their parents' grins were slick with ice.
Living through the first night felt like victory.

On TV that week, brown girls tumbled toward victory.
I called home to my love so he would not be lonely.
When we walked the streets, I ate tea-flavored ice
and told myself this could never be home.
Safia said *They treat us like curiosities*
when the shop owner demanded to know why we were black.

The work of the poet is not unlike the work of being black.
Some days it is no work at all: only ease, cascading victory,
the plentitude of joy and questions and delights and curiosities.
Other days, you wonder if exile would be too lonely
and figure it can't be worse than thinking you won't make it home,
the fear of your own teeth skidding across the ice.

That's what was in my head as I read aloud, as tiny fuzzy halos of ice
began to spread like fingers across the display cases. Jayson tugged his black
sweater tighter around his frame, and I thought of Chicago, my home
where January is so cold that just breathing is adequate victory.
No one else seemed to notice the snow blowing through the door, and I felt suddenly lonely.
I ceased reading and looked for a place to hide from the crowd and their curiosities.

Now there was a steady snowfall, and the host yawned, like he was accustomed to such curiosities.
I pressed my hand to the pane of glass nearest to me and it began to melt under my palm, like ice.
When the glass was all gone, there stood the fur suit, looking bedraggled and lonely.
Squinting in the blizzard, I pulled the suit on. The lights dimmed, then cut out, leaving the room all black.
Fishing in the pocket of the suit, I found a matchbox and lit one. Its glow in the wind was a tiny victory.
Pushing the fur of the hood away from my mouth, I called to my friends in the darkness. *Let's go home.*

We held hands and watched the others turn to ice, their silhouettes hazy and black.
I peered at them, curious as to why they would not move. Maybe their stubbornness called this victory.
Hanif said *Forget it.* The four of us held hands and we trudged homeward, together in our cold and lonely.

True Stories about Koko Taylor

Koko Taylor walked up on John Henry
took the hammer right out his hand
and bent it and twisted it into a fine necklace
and took him to a real nice dinner.

Koko Taylor had twelve thousand wigs.
One she never wore. Just kept at home.
Was enchanted, spun from gold and full of rubies,
and sang to her at night in the voice of her mother.

Koko Taylor wrote songs with a blue ink pen.
Koko Taylor wrote rivers with a blue ink pen.
Koko Taylor wrote the Illinois Central rail line with a blue pen.
Just got right on her knees and scratched it into the ground.

Koko Taylor was the ghostwriter of seventeen Beatles songs.
Koko Taylor was the inventor of the icebox.
Koko Taylor could play chess with checkers.
Koko Taylor could bake a pound cake in the palm of her hand by winking.

Koko Taylor flew from Memphis to Chicago on a jukebox.
The jukebox could grant three wishes.
Koko Taylor wished for lipstick the color she saw in a dream.
She wished to be born again, under a good sign.
She wished for a better jukebox.

I WANTED A MAP
NOT TO KNOW
WHERE THINGS ARE
BUT TO KNOW
WHERE I AM

another time [a re-telling]

I was in Harvard Square, on my way to a meeting. I was walking down Brattle and she was in front of a pizza and salad place that was pretty good. As I passed, she looked at me and furrowed her brow so that her eyes were squeezed up and her nose wrinkled. "Ugh! You nigger." Before I could reply, she was possessed by a mighty and exuberant ghost-spirit. She stood up and began to dance despite herself, kicking and jumping and spinning here and there, hollering, turning cartwheels that made her bones creak and her dress turn upside-down, throwing her hands to the sky and calling out to no one. I kept walking.

Note from LeBron James to LeBron James

I knew it was you when I saw you in the parking lot,
headphones on, waiting for Dru to come up with the car
& trying not to eat all the chips before he got there,
the tip of each finger of each hand
finding its own minute ridged seam on the waistband of your shorts.

I knew it was you from the way you smiled
when you saw how lean my shoulders,
how spare my triceps. I knew it was you because
you haven't yet seen what will come after:
the days when I was a ballast for every vessel I blinked at,
an impossible man,
when I was not the leg lift or the quick step or the hoist:
I was the tire, the hurdle, the rope itself.
I was the trial itself. And you can't
know that yet.

Leaning against nothing there in the sunlight,
me kicking at sticky black pebbles sprung loose from the tar
while you stood firm in your new shoes, a few inches up on the curb
where the melting street couldn't sully them,
and both of us wanting lunch and touching our hips absentmindedly
and listening to a jet pass overhead, the hum of a Saturday,
and looking down the road toward where Portage Path would be,
except too far past the oaks to see, and us not really thinking about that anyway,
I couldn't tell you:

'When it's time to roll you have to keep everybody tethered to you
no matter how heavy or hungry or ugly they get.
You have to keep their soreness and their worst parts
and their smashed tin wants and their construction paper crowns
and their everything they ever wanted for you and for them
in the same backpack with the shredded bottom where you keep
your own drawings and scraped knuckles and your being afraid.
Keep them like a secret.'

I couldn't tell you that just then.

Excerpts from an Interview with Metta World Peace, a.k.a. Ron Artest, a.k.a. the Panda's Friend

yes, I am the Red Storm. that's why I made your eyes hurt.
that's why your shirt is that color now.

Queensbridge is me. I am the stone path over the water
from one monarch to the next,
trodden by ladies-in-waiting with rubies for eyes.

because the old world order was trash. next question?

175. 193. 167. 69. 298. 29.

an elbow is just a bent arm with some ambition
and if you can't handle that why are you playin ball?

because in the 1920s, right before the crash,
they knew what we didn't about the hiss
of things, the buzz of things, how to catch the noise
between noises and that telepathy was real.
and that comes through in their music,
do you know what I mean?
that music that comes from right before you fall
and land hard.

how I arrived

1.
in flight from a war for my own holy self,
clinging to a steamship.

the old farmhouse one day fell in cinders
but today, first, burned into my corneas
still visible when I close my eyes.
a tangerine aura with no center.

I told them I would not fight.

2.
they mailed me from Mississippi
in a metal ice chest.

I taste salt at the sight of honeysuckle,
recalling some kind of way
the last bacon grease to touch
the back of my hand.

I danced, once
from Alabama westward
the longest cakewalk.

3.
I rode in on a bumblebee.

4.

I fell out of the dirt.

5.

I disguised myself as a painter in a time of artless men.

6.

I remember every note you ever wrote to me.

7.

when you pull all day from the coldest water you can find
and do not mind carrying your bicycle up the stairs,

July twilight comes so late
you might forget to end the day at all.

oil and water

Shea Butter Manifesto

We, the forgotten Delta people,
the dry riverbed people,
hair calling always for rain,
skin turned skyward wishing for clouds,
we stand for blood.
We kneel for water.
For oil, we lay down,
fingers spread, as if in this way
we might skate across the yellow clay of it all
like lagoon insects.

So it is written:
heal yourself, baby.
With the tree and the touch, with the turmeric.
In this world, nothing brittle prevails,
so in this world, grease is a compliment,
no, it's a weapon,
no, it's a dream you had, where it was cold
and your mother, seeing the threat of gray at your elbows
and knowing that ash is the language of the dead
knelt, and put her hands on your face like this
and anointed you a protected child, a hot iron in a place of frost.
Recall this, and
fear no thickness.
Be resurrected, glistening in the story of you.
Be shining.

appletree

[on black womanhood, from and to Erykah Badu]

first.

The year *Baduizm* came out
was the same year I had sex ed for the first time.
Not the kind with feelings or warnings or photographs.
It was the vocabulary kind of sex ed,
the kind with diagrams and purple-inked ditto lines.
I was bad at remembering which words
went with which shapes on the page,
and so at school I learned that my body was a worksheet,
full of blank spaces and mysterious, menacing forms,
and the best I could hope
was that someone more knowledgeable than I was
would know what to do with them.

When I came home every day,
my mother would be playing the CD on repeat.
You would begin, and begin again,
Oh, what a day, and I would sigh along with you.
And it was the first time I understood that the violet waxy blobs of my insides
were circles spun with a lazy finger.
There's a small sun in there, you said. A cup of tea.
There's a stone that moves of its own volition,
tracing a path each day from my throat
to the soles of my feet and back up,
across the muscles of my thighs,

over my spine. It's a boulder without a Sisyphus.
I learned that everything about me could be round and full if I let it,
that under my skin were cyphers of humming and laughing and buzzing,
stones laid in a labyrinth that turns and turns in on itself
so when you get to the center
you have no choice but to turn around and walk the other way.
What a day, what a day.

second.

A man can be many things: a snare drum,
or a willow tree with its branches dragging down into muddy water,
the white rind of a watermelon, or a run in your stockings,
or the moment when you see your name
written on the inside of a desk at school
and it wasn't you who wrote it.

But you can be your own gin
and your own best sip too.
You can make with him a nation and still be sovereign,
your own gold coin and your own honest trade.
You can touch his hand
and still be your own snapping fingers
when the snare has gone quiet.

third.

Every black woman is an artist
versed in the craft of the swift,
the game of the subtle,

the gift of the sideways glance.

fourth.

Sometimes being an artist means walking faster than everybody,
shedding your clothes
like the devil had dressed you in his own best ideas,
looking out a window for a long time before you realize
it's got no glass and the wind has been hurting your cheeks,
taking a shot to the heart even as you're called heartless,
asking only for a long farewell
and not getting even that much,
no matter if you asked nice or not.

fifth.

let it go
let it go
let it go
let it go

sixth.

If he don't ever buy you nothing
and I mean *nothing*—
I don't mean your birthstone.
I don't mean groceries, even—
I mean if he don't buy you an ice-cream cone,
I mean if he don't buy you time when you had none,
I mean if he don't buy your fantastic tales, calls them nonsense,

then he's gotta go.

Let me be clear:
there's nothing wrong with finding rapture in the broke
or the broken.
But what you should ask for is a place on the park bench
where all the bits and pieces are everywhere,
and he should hand you the bottom of a smashed-up Coke bottle
like the best kaleidoscope
and you should hold it up to the light together
and watch the colors turn and spin,
and that is more than good enough
until you can get the groceries together.

seventh:

Dear Erykah:
When I was in New Orleans and it was three in the morning
and you still had not come,
and I was so tired, my feet so sore that I could not stand,
my voice hoarse from fighting over whether to give up and go home,
I stayed anyway.
I leaned against a cement pillar like a forgotten bag of rice,
closing my eyes and wondering if this had ever been you—heavy
and empty and over it
in shoes you knew you shouldn't have worn.

And then, like a bass line in a silent room, there you were
slouchy and wide-eyed, twenty feet tall,
in a red t-shirt with Harriet Tubman's face on it.
Yes—you dared bring our Moses into a crowded club
as if to say,

32

even if your namesake was a woman
who broke the limb, who ate the rules,
you are emancipated already, child,
because it was your appletree all along.
It was you, appletree, all along.

I saw it in the bathtub
I thought it was a spider but
it was my hair

what I mean when I say
I'm sharpening my oyster knife

I mean I'm here
to eat up all the ocean you thought was yours.
I mean I brought my own quarter of a lemon,
tart and full of seeds. I mean I'm a tart.
I'm a bad seed. I'm a red-handled thing
and if you move your eyes from me
I'll cut the tender place where your fingers meet.

I mean I never met a dish of horseradish I didn't like.
I mean you're a twisted and ugly root
and I'm the pungent, stinging firmness inside.
I mean I look so good in this hat
with a feather
and I'm a feather
and I'm the heaviest featherweight you know.
I mean you can't spell anything I talk about
with that sorry alphabet you have left over from yesterday.

I mean
when I see something dull and uneven,
barnacled and ruined,
I know how to get to its iridescent everything.
I mean I eat them alive.

what I mean is I'll eat you alive,
slipping the blade in sideways, cutting nothing
because the space was always there.

"No, I do not weep at the world—I am too busy sharpening my oyster knife."
  —_Zora Neale Hurston_

to Stacey, as you were

you pout, golden and annoyed.
you glow all funny, in the way something can be an unexpected beautiful,
like when someone leaves out a can of orange pop
and slowly, slowly emerges a wasp, soothing itself on sugar
reclining on aluminum in the sun as its legs dry.
we're all caught up in this now and I don't know if you're the wasp,
or the can, or the sugar, or the sun
but I know how anxious you look against the leather.

it's black leather. in a black car. and you're a black girl
running because no jet will wait for you,
your heels clicking and your hair dancing
like black-girl hair doesn't dance,
swish on your shoulder blades. we can't hear it for real but
swish your dress, *switch* your hips.
but the tear, when it comes, is silent.

this is how I will remember you, Stacey Lauretta of the Bronx,
Stacey the first woman my brother ever publicly proclaimed love for,
Stacey fabulous hats, Stacey braids, best of the black best friends.

Stacey, best friend that talks about you at the lunch table
or on television.
Stacey, best friend that leaves
but can still come back.

why you cannot touch my hair

my hair is my childhood friend who used to come over every day and became cool in high school and then began to do drugs and then ran away but now is back trying to get her life together and we have coffee together one Sunday morning before her shift at the grocery store

my hair was in a zoo. my hair escaped from the zoo and took out three officers of the law before they shot my hair up full of tranquilizers. tranquilizers only because my hair is too valuable to die

my hair is a speakeasy. it's not that no one can get in—it's just that you don't know the password

my hair did a lot of work and climbed many mountains, literal and metaphorical, to get here. my hair ran out of oxygen tanks a mile back and has been heaving for breath ever since but is determined to reach the summit. my hair endured a bonnet last night. that's a lot of work

my hair is a technology from the future and will singe your fingertips, be careful

my hair doesn't care about what you want

my hair has a brother. I washed and conditioned and moisturized and combed and braided my hair's brother in the kitchen sink when my hair's brother was depressed. my hair's brother has a daughter. my hair's brother's daughter is tenderheaded and I sing while I comb her, holding her at the roots, touching her forehead so gently and telling her I love her while she cries

Ode to Luster's Pink Oil

you'd be a stranger today, ostentatious
between the earth tones and the eggshells
on the Walgreens shelf.
you do not call yourself any kind of butter,
nor are you *free* of anything:
paraben-   sulfate-   hassle-   free.
no, friend. you cost.

> the slick of you and the smell of sugar and hot plastic
> persists with the hands, so some strategy is required
> to protect the jeans, the counter, the cornea, the favorite sweater
> from the telltale stain of a hasty morning and a careless
> flick of the wrist.

you bear no strange tongues.
no, you only know the name of your father.
Luster.
a man of luminous roots.
a man so South Side that in his mouth
Yazoo City, Mississippi rang out
as an anagram of *medium and coarse hair*
and it sounded real nice
cause it was coated with you
and O, how you shine.

one thousand and one ways to touch your own face

1.

I have just come from the Tilt-A-Whirl.
I have three dollars to spend at the gift shop.
the whole ride home
I palm the small tin of eyeshadow,
coiled as it is in the crevice between turquoise
and electric blue
with extra electric,
and when Colette finds me climbing atop the sink to reach the mirror
she tells me,
'if you wear that you'll look like you don't know how to do your makeup.
you'll look like Mrs. Porcelli.'
and helps me down and takes me to the living room
to say hello to Mrs. Porcelli,
my grandmother's next-door neighbor these thirty years,
and to have a glass of flat ginger ale.

2.

'fourteen?' Paula says to me.
'you wear too much makeup for fourteen.'
the boy nearby,
the one I like so much,
the aspiring playwright with grand ideas,
laughs his hardest, and if I were a nailbiter
this would be the time to be a nailbiter with gusto
but I'm not, so the metallic violet ice

at the tip of each finger stays intact.
I turn my orange-caked lids toward her and say nothing.

3.
toward the angry end of fifteen I stopped changing the colors daily.
instead I smeared my lids in black each morning
and wore lipstick
and that was that.
my face bore no pockmarks,
so I wore no powder.

my stomach, though, erupted with my father's inheritance.
beneath my shirt it was all scales and holes, a desert,
or it was a distant, loathed moon,
or it was the beach in winter.
I showed a girl once, in the library.
when she curled her lip
I chastised myself for forgetting how monstrous.

in New York City I told the English woman
that my mother did not like it,
and she said 'your mother
is not supposed to like your makeup.'
and I was fifteen and going
from Harlem to Brooklyn with no parents
and I knew what she said
sounded forbidden and gorgeous, but I thought,
'and here I believed you knew my mother so well.'

the coal compacts I bought

in furtive trips to Walgreens just after sunrise.
the rest I took from her bedroom—
assuming, as was my habit, that her every secret thing
was equally mine.

4.
even now, in this room, I see her
resplendent in indigo, smelling of otherworldly things,
draped in damask before the mirror
as a wandering woman would be,
smiling from the end of a tinkerer's cart,
toes tracing lines luxuriantly through the mud.

5.
my grandmother paid me back
after each trip to Carson Pirie Scott
to fetch the pink-and-green Fashion Fair.
she is eighty-five years old and terrible in her beauty:
a tiny empress,
smiling always and never.
when she sees us dance
she laughs and her eyes widen, tremendous,
and I wonder why mine are so narrow
and I wonder at her secret things
and I wonder if they are mine.

to the notebook kid

yo chocolate milk for breakfast kid.
one leg of your sweatpants rolled up
scrounging at the bottom of your mama's purse for
bus fare and gum
pen broke and you got ink on your thumb kid

what's good, hot on the cement kid
White Castle kid
tongue stained purple
cussin on the court
til your little brother shows up
with half a candy bar kid

got that good B in science kid
you earned it kid
etch your name in a tree
hug your granny on her birthday
think of Alaska when they shootin
curled-up dreams of salmon
safety
tundra
the farthest away place you ever saw in a book
polar bears your new chess partners
pickax in the ice
Northern Lights kid

keep your notebook where your cousins won't find it.
leave it on my desk if you want

shuffle under carbon paper
and a stamp that screams LATE
yellow and red to draw the eye from the ocean
you keep hidden in a jacked-up five-star.
your mama thought there was a secret in there
thought they would laugh
but that ain't it.

it's that flows and flows and flows
and lines like those rip-roaring
bits you got
bars till the end of time
you could rap like
helium bout to spring
all of it
down to you
none left in the sun—fuelless
while the last light pushes from your belly

climbing your ribs

and you laugh into the microphone

and who is ready for that?

Thursday Morning, Newbury Street

I can't afford this therapist.

He sees me for a nominal amount—so low that when he first names the number I ask to pay ten dollars more. So low that it is really just a courtesy. It's symbolic, like the city selling vacant lots for a dollar. Can't do nothing with that money. He says it is "part of his practice" to see one or two students at a time. It seems to me like a sort of tithe, a donation to the universe to say "thank you for these degrees and this office and this midcentury modern furniture and these orchids in this building on Newbury Street."

Other times I think he just keeps me on because my problems are so interesting and sometimes involve names that are maybe not famous per se, but suffice it to say they are names you would know if you were a highly educated black therapist with an office on Newbury Street. Or maybe it's not the sordid tales of the black intelligentsia; maybe it's my vivid storytelling, or my willingness to say "I don't see it that way," or maybe I'm kidding myself and it's just the regular stories of poor people trying to make do in poor times and the things they do that are maybe not so good for their baby girlchildren but everyone is trying to get by and the girlchildren don't even have a chance to think about it too much until they are living in a faraway city. Or maybe the man is just doing his job. These are not the kinds of questions you can ask so I probably will never know.

Whatever it is, I am grateful. When I say *it took me a week but finally I watched the video of her getting pulled over / I feel afraid to get in my car* and he nods I am grateful. When I tell him how they put black tape on the portraits of the black Harvard Law faculty, right over the eyes, I cry and am grateful not to explain. Eventually I come to realize that in therapy, as in much of life, the things that cost more money are actually better and I am receiving better care than I have from any of my previous five therapists. I don't know who to feel sorry for, me or them.

I take mid-day appointments when I can. Most of the time when I leave the office there is no one in the anteroom, waiting. I take my coat and leave. Sometimes I do my makeup in the bathroom.

Sometimes someone is in the room, waiting their turn. They are always white. I wonder what they talk about, and who they are, and if they say well-meaning but uncomfortable things ever. Things about the news, about hair, about fear, about death. I think of colleagues I know who call me and only me "girlfriend," who say "word" to show agreement with me and only me, and I wonder if that kind of zeal enters this office or if therapists are immune to small indignities by virtue of knowing everything terrible about you.

Every once in a while there is a nervous-looking white child—a different one every time—with an adult who is reading a magazine and not speaking to him. I smile and say hello because the room is small and anyway aren't we supposed to make this as normal as possible? Or, ma'am, would you like me to help your child feel uncomfortable being here? Shall I show him that this is a secret? There is never enough time to read the social cues before acting. So I err toward the awkward smile, especially in winter when it takes a long time to gather my coat and we're all just in this tiny chamber, listening to jazz and feeling ashamed to be crazy. As I wait for the elevator I always imagine the child sitting at the miniature wooden table at one end of the office, playing Connect Four with Dr. ////. He is tall and I imagine him folding in half to squeeze into a handsomely crafted, catalogue-ordered Eames chair. I feel envious that my therapy does not involve board games. I wonder at what moment in the game of Chinese Checkers the child reveals that which is hidden.

It is my last in-person appointment before I move home, but I am so forcibly uncomfortable with departures that I act like it is not. We will have some Skype sessions, anyway. To ease the transition. Mostly I feel like I can't afford to have this be another thing that makes me cry. But part of the video calls will be to help me find someone new. My mother asks constantly what will happen with my therapist. I won't call her any kind of convert. She is not completely immune from the many forces that would convince black women that mental health is a farce at worst and a luxury at best. But the idea of therapy is, like math and the dentist, the kind of thing she was flatly denied for most of her life and yet is adamant that I pursue relentlessly. She is pleased when I tell her that I am not saying goodbye, not just yet. I report this on the phone in the slightly disingenuous way that a child reports a good grade on an assignment that was actually pass/fail. It is a technical truth.

Dr. //// and I do not hug. We shake hands.

And today when I walk out, there is a black boy. We mirror one another, dressed alike except that he is wearing a snapback and I am not. We look at each other, wide-eyed, before Dr. //// opens the door and invites him in. When it is shut, I am not supposed to be able to hear anything. That is what the jazz is for. But I hear very well. I hear the smooth sound of skin against skin, first the slip of the palms and then the gentle thud. I hear them greet one another in the way they can, the way no one else can.

I think that maybe if we can guard ourselves and each other, if we can keep from losing our minds alone in quiet rooms and can at least lose them side by side, we may live through the year.

letters from the flatlands

On Prince

In 1990 I would sit alone in the kitchen and eat Jell-O
and I would speak along with you when you promised:
don't worry
I won't hurt you
and my delirious synthesizer heart
would go *kuh kuh kuh kuh* in my ribcage,
until it was over and I had to rewind
fast, or be alone again.
I didn't know what a Corvette was but I knew it was small
and that it made you sad, and I wanted to have a
trembling, breaking voice like that, and I wanted
a motorcycle and something to be sad about.
I wanted to play guitar with the rain falling
all off my body, and shake my shoulders when I walked.
See, I loved you because I had never seen
someone in a movie that looked like me before,
or at least how I thought I could look
if I grew up to be beautiful.
Our same skin, always shining,
adorned with every kind of taffeta
and smooth curls, falling perfectly around my face
like they were drawn there.
That was my secret revolution.
I would have fought Morris Day if you asked,
hitting him with small fists and watching the gold
in his jacket yield and bend until it went dull.
It wasn't lost on me that they gave Joker your color
when he stormed the place, signing his name to everything

they had called art. He twirled a scepter,
defaced what he could, and smashed the rest.
They should have had you there, or me,
dancing amidst the plaster clouds and sullied canvas.
And I knew then
that 1999 would never come,
and we would always be here among the organs.
And there was never a music video for that song,
but if there was I wanted to be the one
with a lion in my pocket,
and it wouldn't be a tiny lion or a giant pocket
but just a special filthy cute magic
that made the most fearsome things my friends,
and made my hands strong.

Origin Story

This is true:
my mother and my father
met at the Greyhound bus station
in the mid-eighties in Chicago.
my mother, all thick glass and afro puff,
came west on the train when she was nineteen,
lived in a friend's house and cared for her children,
played tambourine in a Chaka Khan cover band.
my father, all sleeveless and soft eye,
ran away from home when he was seventeen,
mimeographed communist newspapers
and drew comic books
like this one, for sale. one dollar.
my mother bought one.

love is like a comic book. it's fragile
and the best we can do is protect it
in whatever clumsy ways we can:
plastic and cardboard, dark rooms
and boxes. in this way, something
never meant to last
might find its way to another decade,
another home, an attic, a basement, intact.
love is paper.
and if my parents' love was a comic book,
it never saw polyvinyl, never felt a backing.
it was curled into a back pocket for a day at the park,
lent to a friend, read under covers,

reread hanging upside-down over the back of the couch,
memorized, mishandled, worn thin, staples rusted.
a love like that doesn't last
but it has a good ending.

sonnet

after Terrance Hayes

I saved some cornbread for you in the skillet on the stove.
I saved some cornbread for you in the skillet on the stove.
I saved some cornbread for you in the skillet on the stove.
I saved some cornbread for you in the skillet on the stove.

I saved some cornbread for you in the skillet on the stove.
I saved some cornbread for you in the skillet on the stove.
I saved some cornbread for you in the skillet on the stove.
I saved some cornbread for you in the skillet on the stove.

I saved some cornbread for you in the skillet on the stove.
I saved some cornbread for you in the skillet on the stove.
I saved some cornbread for you in the skillet on the stove.
I saved some cornbread for you in the skillet on the stove.

I saved some cornbread for you in the skillet on the stove.
I saved some cornbread for you in the skillet on the stove.

Chicago is a chorus of barking dogs

[Logan Square, night, May 30, 2015]

[a. notes on the sonic biosphere]

It's not like I had forgotten. But I didn't rightly remember, either.
Not from a distance. Not in the way that I do when you are next to me, asleep,
and they are right outside your window: first only one, then three,
then more than I can count, though I try to see each one with my eyes closed:
a pitbull, a shih tzu, a wide-headed mutt, arrayed across the gangway
as though lining the back of the stage—one voice, one warning, though they are many.
You don't stir. Even when the woman upstairs begins to scream,
throwing things and shouting every name for the worthless.

[b. notes on your parentage]

Watching you breathe through the billowing, bellowing vapor that is the place we are from,
I remember a name for you: *my Division Street baby,*
a Blue Line baby in a redlined city,
a black and white and brown baby. A Cabrini-Green Studs Terkel Clemente baby.
You're a metal flag and a wig shop, my darling.
On that merit alone I don't mind sharing this thirty-six-inch-wide not-a-bed with you
since, good as you are at sleeping through the dogs and the fury,
I'm that good at making it a whole night without moving an inch.
And when you call out in the night, I'll call back.

[c. notes on the nature of lungs, a blueprint]

My brother, your father, is supposed to work until four tonight.

When I hear the door early I listen—not for any sort of footfall.
I'm waiting for the rasp. The involuntary snort. If the night walker moves air in silence
it's not my brother. But the rattling breath comes quickly enough
and I know it's him.

[d. notes on 18th street and death and green glass]

On my way to the bathroom he asks me if I remember Rudy,
our father's friend who maybe lived above the Jumping Bean,
was nice and gave him Trix. In this moment I understand
that in the head and heart of my brother, as in my own head and my own heart,
to give the gift of food, and particularly forbidden sugary food, and particularly
forbidden sugary cereal, is to have a home always. And I am not surprised at this.
And he tells me that Rudy was stabbed to death tonight, in Simone's.
I say something stupid like
a lot of people in Pilsen are named Rudy and maybe it's not the same guy
but I know it is. And in Simone's, where I have been so often, so I can see the whole thing.
The next day on the phone my father will be angry at the news calling it an *altercation*,
insisting that Rudy would never fight anybody. He calls it an ambush
and I won't have anything to say then and I don't have anything to say now.

[e. anticlimax, in defense of communion]

My brother says he is trying to get you into the habit of sleeping alone,
and that if you wake up he'll attend to you. He gives me another clean blanket
and I leave you, reluctantly, for the couch.
Our own dog, skinny and quiet, sleeps nearby. Upstairs someone flushes a toilet,
sending water rushing in a great invisible cascade through the wall.
I wonder what it was like for people who grew up without the noise of other people—
if as adults they have to grow used to the sounds of others living and dying

or if it comes naturally, like something their senses have always been waiting for.
Like right now his door is open, and yours is,
and I hear you both breathing, not having a door myself,
and for the first time I realize that for the first third of my years
I never slept in a different room from this person whose lungs have worried me my whole life
as if they were my own delicate dilemma.
And I think of you, and the music you make in this house of jilted breath,
and I open my eyes when you call for your father, my brother,
and I listen when he calls back and comes for you.
Girl child, you fearless winter,
you gathering of pigeons before a lasting fountain—
we don't want you to be afraid of the dark like we were.
We want you to be able to be alone sometimes
the way we never could and still can't really.
But who can blame you, baby, in our city of glass?

at the salon

sorry baby
says Miss Annetta as she pulls
my head by my hair, through plastic,
and sees my jaw flex,
and muscles in my neck that had been invisible.

soon I am in a house
no, I am in an ocean
no, I am plasma in the sun
no, I am an atom in a particle accelerator
and time is so slow for me. I don't know it.
and before me the whole universe is here
like the closing scenes of Kubrick:
vast and flowing and
did you know glass is a liquid?
it's moving before your eyes but too slow to see.
that's what this is.
I am in the universe and it is my hair.
each strand arched electric and perfectly still
before my eyes, dancing, crooked,
arranged just so in the air
like the last humming chord of a song.
I watch them from inside. one is white,
twisting amidst the others like a bolt of quiet lightning.
she tugs some more and now I am a veiled woman.
I see the world from here, and the world is dark brown,
and the world keeps me modest, hidden.
from without, I am not a face, but a lace curtain

as over a woman betrothed
as over the window of a solemn neighbor
as over a passing hearse
I sit a little taller, for one so hidden
must be of consequence.
she combs again and I see again:
the dryers, the flickering television
the OPEN sign through which men sometimes peer,
eyes finding gaps in the neon as they pass in the street.

montage in a car.

I am two I am in a car seat my mother and my grandfather have gone to pick up photos from a drive-through pharmacy they complain because the photos are not ready I say 'are you angry?' // I am four my father says 'damn it' I say 'Dad' // I am ten reading the classifieds in the last section of a *Reader* my father left in the back seat there are many women with no shirts on // I am eleven and we are going to a neighborhood where I have never been to stay with a woman I have never met because we cannot go home anymore all of my books and stuffed animals are in a box beside me I am hot // I am twelve coming to the last page of *Flowers for Algernon* sobbing silently while we cross the Allegheny Mountains // I am sixteen the snow is so bad all we can see are the red lights of a truck in front we follow without knowing where it is going on the side of the road are so many dead cars covered all covered up and tracks leading into the woods // I am fourteen I say where are we going he says it's a surprise // I am seventeen the Remix to 'Ignition' is playing he is smoking a cigarette out the window I keep my window down too we look at Christmas lights it is two in the morning // I am twenty-three this battery is dead there is nothing I can do I gun it to the top of the ramp put my hazards on and coast into the right lane just let it happen // I am twenty-five I don't know where anything in Cambridge is yet I call his best friend and say he is so drunk I had to leave tell me what to do I call Lo he tells me to come over I don't come over // I am twenty-eight it is raining I scream 'I will kill us I will kill us both' // I am twenty-nine we are going back to Pilsen from New Harmony the moon is high I stop they are both asleep they are grown but look like babies when we were babies our problems were grown they do not wake up even when I cut the ignition and step out into the night

The Discount Megamall (in memoriam)

for you
i trace
the
letters
of my
name
in the
air
with my
pinky
like a
gold
necklace
like a
signature
on a
grain
of rice
in a
little jar
eve
the night
before
like a
dusk
like
the end
of things beloved

I come from the fire city.

i come from the fire city / fire came and licked up our houses, lapped them up like they were nothing / drank them like the last dribbling water from a concrete fountain / the spigot is too hot to touch with your lips be careful / fire kissed us and laughed / and even now the rust climbs the walls, red ivy / iron fire and the brick blossoms florid / red like stolen lipstick ground down to a small flat earth / stand on any corner of the fire city, look west to death / the red sun eats the bungalows / the fire city children watch with their fingers in their mouths / to savor the flaming hots or hot flamins or hot crunchy curls or hot chips / they open the fire hydrants in the fire city and lay dollar store boats in the gutters / warrior funeral pyres unlit

Hood Run: A Poem in Five Acts

Act I: The Van
What's going into or out of or through

this van that it's got to be parked halfway up
on the sidewalk when the sidewalk here is just
rubble anyways so I have to choose
between scraping my elbow on the wall of the laundromat
and maybe tripping on the loose stones for good measure
or step into the street to get hit
by a car or the rusted door of the van
or hollered at by you, the van driver, who put me in this real tight spot.

Act II: The Ketchup and the Glass
The glass I expect. I can jump the glass in all its forms,
the calling card of other nights
and other runners of a different sort,
other tracks and other burning insides.
Each time in the moment I feel my hamstring stretch extra
to send me in the smallest orbit over the shards
that in their way were garbage before they were even trash, before they were even broken,
I see myself in two visions—here I fly
and here I miss, landing with the glass in my knee or my shin,
and it's the second mind that keeps my soles flexed in the right way.

The ketchup is a surprise—twelve or fifteen packets at least,
none intact, but they're everywhere, and ketchup is everywhere,
no fries or anything or paper plates or other signs
that a good time was had by anybody,

and as my muscles tighten and I push off
I wonder if it was a mother, or a jilted lover,
who came home with the glory of McDonald's dinner
but found the one waiting to be so unworthy
that all his gifts should be left here to dry in the sun.

Act III: The Snake
Let me tell you,
this little fool rearin up on me
like he forgot whose garden this really was.
Tryna play with me like you know somethin.
You must of lost yo natural mind.
You ain't gon bite nobody!
Act like you got
some sense.

Act IV: The Men
are not so bad but still to be avoided.
The name of this game is how quick is your quick-turn
on your heel when he comes into view,
how to set the volume on your headphones
so you don't have to fake not hearing but can actually not hear
and yet won't be caught unawares by someone sneaking up on you
[they don't make headphones like that yet
but we could make a mint off women who insist on going outdoors],
how much do you mind
when you don't see his arm out the driver's side of the parked car
until you're right up on it,

and how grateful are you when he just says 'hey, slim' and nothing worse.

Act V: The Playground
_____ is my playground
is how you say this is the place I come to show out
with no fear, like as though I had never caught a woodchip in my knee
or got burned by a metal slide or stung by a wasp
living between the molding planks of the sandbox.
As in, the city is my playground. As in, the playground is my playground
and I hopscotch like I never heard of foursquare
and foursquare like I never heard of a bad knee.
As in, this ain't a place for kids
who heave their bodies off the swings and land face-first
but haven't learned yet how to heave with the whole chest
like it's their last day on a dying planet and no one brought
the oxygen tanks.

one good time
for Marilyn Mosby

Dorchester girl gold necklace
heavy on your heart like
your blue eyed blue heart Grandma
Mosby like that Southern kind of song
gone to the Shawmut Peninsula
with your blue chest blue head daddy like
one of the good ones daddy like
I got this handshake from my daddy like
this is the most
belonging you ever got with this suit, at this podium:
the day they all gathered to hear you count them
like a desperate man counts a pistol's hailing
one through six, timpani mallets bang heavy on his heart like
his spine heavy on your heart like
a broken pencil snapped jagged
not even in anger—in heedlessness
by a heavy heel, and abandoned.
your eyebrows furrow till your face is the jagged graphite
they love to spit at. they count your sniffles
and gasps. they whittle your yell, in their heads.
they pull the compass to the curl of your lips
and howl at each defiant degree.
When you say 'probable' and 'contrary' and 'dispatch'
they measure the gap in your teeth with their high school rings.
They don't like the flip of your hair, Mari.
They don't like your lip gloss.

They don't like how sharp your knife was
when you slid it between the pewter eagle
and the blue polyester fabric
and sliced
and they don't like how you folded it back into itself
and laid it on the asphalt.

Columbus Hospital

The first stone is the hardest
which is why they don't use hands anymore.
Too much, the push of the granite on the pads of the fingers
too much like the push of a match on the side of the dollar-store box
when the phosphorus has all gone out of it, the tinder has all gone
out of its heart, and the red is scratched with brown such that you
rub and scrape but the fire never comes.
It hurts too much, that fruitless scrape.

So they don't use their hands anymore.
No, the croaking chain does a man's job.
Wrecking balls don't get arthritis or cry
or show up on site with lunches that their wives made,
bleary-eyed, standing in worn housecoats in the darkness.
The dynamite never says "but my uncle died
here, in this hospital, and I still smell the ammonia
and see the misshapen pound cake"
while the tremor spreads
and the walls come down.

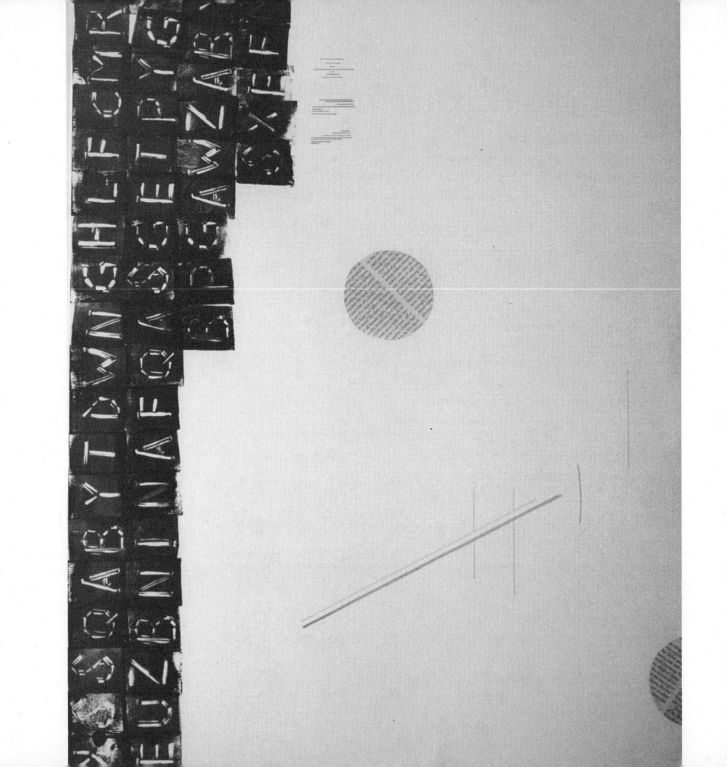

What I Talk About When I Talk About Black Jesus

I mean it when I say *hallelujah.*

I don't believe that Jesus of Nazareth was the holy son of God, or that he died so that mankind could be saved from our sins, or that he was resurrected as our messiah. But I believe in messiahs.

I believe in miracles and hexes, curses and omens, I believe that you should never put your purse on the floor or split a pole, and when I'm feeling aimless I can fall for a little bit of ill-informed astrology. I don't step on cracks. I believe in an infinite, mysterious universe, and I believe that that universe is mostly dark matter, and that one day the sun will implode. And I don't expect that I'll be alive to see it, but if I am, I will look up at that star I have known and loved more than any other star, and I will say "oh, lord Jesus," and I will be talking about Black Jesus.

When I say *hallelujah,* I mean it. I really mean it.

—

Ever since black people came to this country we have needed a Moses. There has always been so much water that needs parting. It seems like all black children, from the time we are born, come into the world in the midst of a rushing current that threatens to swallow us whole if we don't heed the many, many warnings we are told to heed. We come into the world as alchemists of the water, bending it, willing it to bear us safe passage and cleanse us along the way, to teach us to move with joy and purpose and to never, ever stop flowing forward into something grand waiting at the other end of the delta. We're a people forever in exodus.

Before Moses there was Abraham, and ever since black people came to this country we have needed an Abraham. We have always been sending each other away—for our own good, don't you know it—and calling each other back, finding kinship where a well springs from tears. We are masters of the art of sacrifice; no one is more skilled at laying their greatest beloveds on the altar and feeling certainty even as we feel sorrow. And when we see the ram, we know how to act fast, and prosper, even as the stone knife warms in our hands.

And before Abraham there was Eve, my own namesake. The first black woman who ever lived. She was the first person on this strange sunlit planet to know anything at all, though she paid for it with terrible cramps.

But that's the Old Testament. Back to Black Jesus.

—

"Take a picture of that with your phone," my grandma instructs, her slight frame leaning over my own. She is wearing a grandma uniform with which you might be familiar: she has just returned from singing at church and so her makeup and hair are impeccable, and has also changed into a pearl-colored cotton housecoat with faint traces of a floral pattern, and a pair of slippers. I sometimes worry that in our day and age, grandmas have limited places to purchase housecoats, and dwindling numbers of people even know what a housecoat is, leaving them to guard the ones they have left like careful misers. This particular housecoat thrives on against all odds, and rather than clashing with the hair and makeup—one thinning and fading, the other regal and perfect—they exist in a sort of détente. They have tolerated each other for this many years and they might as well keep on keeping on.

"Take a picture of that, too, so you can show your mom." She is showing me the booklet from the church's centennial celebration, featuring photographs of families living and dead, and stories from the last century that she—the official Historian of the centennial committee—had told somebody so that they could write it down and put it in the booklet and people would remember them in another hundred years. And in case they don't—in case booklets and Microsoft Word and printed things have crumbled from our collective sight in the next century—she wants these things to be inside my phone, where they can last forever in the place everyone seems to care about—a vast digital sky, a celestial hive.

My grandma has spent a great deal of her adult life as President of the Shiloh Baptist Church choir, and this fact is the basis upon which rests her authority on innumerable things. She can tell you which potato salad should be ordered where on the long foldout table, who ought to work which shifts at the food pantry, and whether Pastor Sandy's wig is acceptable, and answer endless other crucial questions, each time ending her sentence with "Well, after all, I *am* president of the choir." Even when I was tiny I could hear that she was singing even when she was not singing—no woman could offer you a piece of toast or a glass of ginger ale in such a lilting, untouchable soprano, or tell you that Grandpa was going to hit you with a comb if you didn't settle down and have it sound so like a Wagnerian opera.

My grandma was born on January 1, 1938, in Houston, Mississippi. She is a New Year. She is a gospel reborn in the winter, from a place where there is no winter. She gave me her name—Louise, meaning "warrior"—on May 31, 1986, and we have shared it between us ever since. When she took me to church, I never went to Sunday school. I always stayed by her side or with one of my cousins, nestled against the upholstery and smelling the smell of old wood and of the starch spray lifting up the stiff collars around me. Although I lived 450 miles away, everyone knew my name as though I had been there just last week, knew about what my mother had been up to and about my grades in school. And if someone didn't recognize me, "That's Louise's grandbaby" was all the uninitiated needed to hear.

Of all the hours I have spent in Shiloh Baptist Church, I cannot tell you the message or even the topic of a single sermon. But I can tell you whose grandbaby I am.

At work with my father

Back then there was the ferris wheel
and the 21st-century McDonald's
with the glass orb you can touch and pink lightning
comes to your fingertips like a fruit punch stain
and not much else. You'd barely recognize it.
Navy Pier was a new and desperate thing,
and instead of fireworks a man set himself on fire
and jumped in the water every night at ten, I'm not even kidding.
I'm telling you you'd barely recognize it.
My father built a structure, like a little house or gazebo kind of,
where the Shakespeare Theatre is now. And he painted it blue.
And it was kind of set back, not the best location really
(later he would move inside)
so a lot of times he would draw us to get people to come over
when things were slow, or draw one of us really
while the other watched over his shoulder, which also got people to come over.

You'd think after all that watching I'd be able to do what he does.
I can do the talk—"so where you from? ohhh, okay"—
like it was the most natural thing, like he talked to people all the time.
I can make the bad jokes. But I can't do the drawing.
He finds cheekbones and the patterns on your shirt
and makes you look coyly at your husband even if really you're indifferent.
I can't do any of that but I do have a lot of airbrushed drawings of myself,
with all the different glasses I ever had and sometimes with invented details,
like binoculars around my neck during my ornithology phase,
or with an "as if!" hand extended, palm upward, during my irreverent teen years.
I've stacked them all carefully, in their original polyvinyl bags

with their original backing boards, nestled among old love letters
which I suppose they also are, in their way.

I cannot draw my father, with invented details or even real ones.
No, my childish love note was the night spent in the crowd
watching the boats come in, selling glow sticks to pass the time,
Making chains of them and hanging them on my skinny arms by the dozen,
yelling at tourists the slogans I invented—*light up the night with a glow light!*
until the time came for the man to climb the pier's cement edge with a torch in hand
while the music blared, an electric guitar with no name,
and I stood silent, gangly and fluorescent
and my father, at the edge of my vision, massaged his aching fingers.

Fullerton Avenue

All I ever really wanted you to know about me
was Fullerton Avenue.

Every time I try to tell you this or tell anyone
the poem ends up on the bottom of my shoe
and I'm stuck.

All I ever really wanted you to know was
when you're driving around looking for a parking spot
and the lighting is all crazy
you suddenly realize how many fire hydrants there really are.

There was no one here, before. No friends.
When I rode the bus to school I could walk back to Kimball and Fullerton
and if I was lucky I would run into the one kid I went to school with who lived in my neighborhood,
a Polish kid who was nice to everybody and would later marry a Mexican girl
and he was pretty nice to talk to there, in front of the laundromat
that was pretty nice too and was not the one we went to.
If Glen wasn't there it was just me.
Once a kid in my art class told me that he was mugged at that bus stop,
which was strange to me, since mugging seemed like something that happens
to old ladies in movies, and if you're young
and someone wants to take your stuff they take it, and that's called you got robbed.

Next to the vein treatment center
my mom got a job at a gym for women after she was sick,
which she called a blessing, and she was right and all but
I never wanted to go in there or look at it for too long.

And once you got to about Albany and Fullerton you could see
every place my brother had been, if you knew where to look.
I loved seeing the name he chose for himself and scrawled for himself
all along the way, because each felt like a silent *hello, hello, hello*.
At the Fireside Bowl I saw Motion City Soundtrack
and there was one other black kid there
and he was the drummer for the opening band
and was really big and to move through the crowd
he held his sticks in the air and said
Excuse me, black guy coming through
which I was too small for and too much of a lot of other stuff too, I guess.
I was brave enough to pass a note to a boy.
In between acts I listened to Wes brag about meeting Karen O
and absentmindedly counted the buttons on the purse I had made myself.

All I ever wanted you to know was that when the landlord got too mean
we had to move further west on Fullerton Avenue, from Sawyer to Kildare
which was past Pulaski
and now I had to take two buses, the 74 and then the 82,
and it took a very long time. I waited in front of the video store that had
titles in Spanish that looked salacious and interesting. I went inside once
looking for a job.
Sometimes I could ride the bus with a boy that lived on my block,
with his grandma. He was sad a lot. Looking back what I wish
was that I could have rode the bus with my brother.
We left at different times to go to different schools and
I wish I could have stood there with him, with his red shirt.

When we lived on Kildare, I never crossed Fullerton Avenue
because I saw the people who waited on the other side

and I heard them at night.
I walked as far west as Cicero, mainly only when I was looking for work.
Mostly I just waited for the bus to go east, tracing the way block
by block back toward apartments I had liked more, where I could
pretend we still lived. By the library
and the YMCA where we went to summer camp
and Tony's Finer Foods
and most of all the boulevard, where my favorite house
had red linen curtains on the second floor
and no one seemed to notice me studying the doorbell year after year.

All I ever wanted you to know was that on the bus
a strange man put his hand on my thigh and I didn't know
if it was really happening or not and still don't. Maybe I made it up.
A boy with fat pupils stood with his teeth against the ear of
another boy and hissed at him: *I know you're a snake.*
The other one stared straight ahead.

On the way home from school if I got off the bus at Kildare
it would be on the right side of the street,
which for me was the wrong side of the street,
so I took to getting off early, crossing, and walking.
There wasn't much to look at except the storage facility,
a towering structure that in theory offered infinite
possibilities—what was inside all those boxes, after all?—
but I couldn't think up much.
Nearby there was an industrial food processing plant
that filled the air with a heavy black pepper smell
which for a while was fascinating or even pleasant—
soup all the time, what a world—then became oppressive.

Trivia: Hermosa means beautiful. Trivia: Walt Disney was born
at 2156 North Tripp and maybe it was all that beauty and all that awful fake pepper
and all those secret boxes that made him
such a fanciful and hateful man,
but who am I to say?

All I ever wanted you to know was
when I smell black pepper I feel sick and lonely, now.

<u>Tuesday</u>
8:30 - Good morning circle
9:00 - I'm raising the children
        you have forgotten.
10:15 - And you have no
         goddamned clue.
11:05 - Lunch
12:10 - Just. Pay Me. Pay me.
12:55 - I refuse to fold my hands.
1:40 - Would you love them
        as your own? As I do?
2:30 - Dismissal

Requiem for Fifth Period
and the Things That Went On Then

Sing, muse, of the science teacher
looking wearily at the stack of ungraded projects
leaning against the back wall, beneath a board on which
she has hastily drawn a pinnate leaf and a palmate leaf
with a violet dry erase marker.
She moves from her desk to the window to watch the flag football game
and the man in an electric wheelchair leaving the senior housing complex
and an old Lincoln Town Car parked near the tremendous pothole that damaged her axle that morning
and the White Castle bag moving in a sudden gust across the basketball court, as if possessed
and Mr. Harris, blowing his whistle.

Tell us of Javonte Stevens, who is in the fourth grade
and who is now tapping Mr. Harris on the shoulder to say
that Miss Kaizer will be sending over three kids
who did not bring in their field trip money
and cannot go to the aquarium
and is that okay.
Sing of Javonte's new glasses,
their black frames and golden hinges that glint in the sun,
and his new haircut, with two notched arrows shorn above his temples
and his new socks which are hidden but which feel best of all
and which were the last of the new things he received from his auntie this weekend
when she visited from Detroit and slept on the couch and declared that
Javonte's improved grades meant that he should have many new things.
Sing of the rough-hewn piece of wood Javonte used
to keep the heavy door ajar while he was outside.

Call out
the noise it made against the painted cement when he kicked it back in.
Sing the song Javonte hummed as he carried his message
back up the stairs, stepping in tune, nodding in tune
to Bo as she called after him,
warning him not to slip on the newly mopped floor.

Sing, muse, of Bo, moving the mop
from the top of the ramp to the bottom,
stepping gingerly past the place where the carpet's unruly corner bends upward,
guiding the wheels of the bucket to stay unwillingly upright
despite the heavy dent in the one.
Speak of the pungent, alkaline smell of the water
and the slap when the fibers hit the floor
and the squeal of the bathroom door
and the shuddering sob,
audible in the moment that disc two of *The Broker* by John Grisham
skips in Bo's CD player,
and her pause in the threshold
and her retreat to the boys' room, which can be cleaned first.

Tell of Nakyla Smith, breathing in sharply when the bathroom door closes,
pushing the stall open gently, silently moving to the sink,
splashing water on her face and wiping her eyes
with the sleeve of her blue oxford.
Sing of her heavy ascent to the counselor's office,
for today is the day
she will unbutton her collar, and the button below, and the button below,
and tug aside the bleached white tank top
to show the small, round burns that pepper her breast.

Praise Ms. Hightower, who does not gasp or cry out at the moment of revelation,
only holds one brown hand in her own
and with her left, lifts the phone and dials Mrs. Marshall,
though she is only just across the hall.

Sing, muse, of Mrs. Marshall, who cannot answer now.
The desk is unattended and she leans
against the other side of the oaken door,
the principal's side, where a sign reads "Children Are My Business"
and a doll-like painted woman smiles broadly, surrounded by the faces of earnest pupils.
She is resting against the wood as her forearms strain
with the weight of all the papers,
colored like oatmeal or dust, each with a label at the top.
The first says STEVENS, JAVONTE, and below that, KAIZER,
and below that, eight numbers.
Tell of how she collates them by classroom, then alphabetically,
though each letter is the same, though each bears the same news.

Tell, muse, of the siren that called their joy sparse and their love vacant.
Tell of the wind that scattered them.

untitled anti-elegy

I   think about

    never let myself

Jonylah Watkins
Jonylah Watkins
Jonylah Watkins

if I do I will
think about how

was your age and I don't want to
for one second

she _ _ _ _ _ have been   _ _ _

I don't want to speak that

Affirmation

to youth living in prison
after Assata Shakur

Speak this to yourself
until you know it is true.

I believe that I woke up today
and my lungs were working,
miraculously,
my voice can sing and murmur and ask,
miraculously.
My hands may shake, but they can hold
me, or another.
My blood still carries the gifts of the air
from my heart to my brain,
miraculously.
Put a finger to my wrist or my temple
and feel it: I am magic. Life
and all its good and bad and ugly things,
scary things which I would like to forget,
beautiful things which I would like to remember
—the whole messy lovely true story of myself
pulses within me.
I believe that the sun shines,
if not here, then somewhere.
Somewhere it rains,
and things will grow green and wonderful.
Somewhere inside me, too, it rains,
and things will grow green and wonderful.
Sometimes my insides rain from the inside out
and then I know
I am alive
I am alive
I am alive

Acknowledgments

Sincere thanks to the editors of the publications in which several of these poems have previously appeared: "to the notebook kid" in *Poetry* and in *The BreakBeat Poets: New American Poetry in the Age of Hip-Hop*, "Requiem for Fifth Period and the Things That Went On Then" in *Bird's Thumb*, "On Prince" in *Drunk in a Midnight Choir*, "Shea Butter Manifesto," "sonnet," and "Arrival Day" in the *Adroit Journal*, "why you cannot touch my hair" in *HEArt*, and "how I arrived" in *Blackberry*. The lyric essay "What I Talk About When I Talk About Black Jesus" first appeared on *Seven Scribes*. The essay "Thursday Morning, Newbury Street" first appeared in the *Indiana Review*.

Thanks to my ancestors. Thanks to my family. Thanks to Damon for everything, always, forever. Thanks to Nate for being a great editor and a better friend. Thanks to Hanif who is the best collective-mate a poet could ask for. Thanks to my unbeatable poetry family: Alex and Amanda and avery and Britteney and Camonghne and Clint and Danez and Diamond and Fati and Febo and Franny and Jamila and Janae and Jason and Jayson and Jerriod and José and Idris and Keith and Kevin and Kiese and Kris and Krista and Kush and Mo and Morgan and Porsha and Ross and RJ and Safia and Sarah and Sofía and Tara and Ydalmi and all the rest of y'all in your infinite splendor. Thanks to Tabia for helping this book find a home in the world. Thank you to Juli, Jim, and everyone at Haymarket Books for believing in this project. Thanks to all the Scribes. And in everything I do I have to thank Abena and Celia and Deepa and Shauna and Steff. I got angels all around me; they keep me surrounded.

about haymarket books

Haymarket Books is a radical, independent, nonprofit book publisher based in Chicago.

Our mission is to publish books that contribute to struggles for social and economic justice. We strive to make our books a vibrant and organic part of social movements and the education and development of a critical, engaged, international Left.

We take inspiration and courage from our namesakes, the Haymarket martyrs, who gave their lives fighting for a better world. Their 1886 struggle for the eight-hour day—which gave us May Day, the international workers' holiday—reminds workers around the world that ordinary people can organize and struggle for their own liberation. These struggles continue today across the globe—struggles against oppression, exploitation, poverty, and war.

Since our founding in 2001, Haymarket Books has published more than five hundred titles. Radically independent, we seek to drive a wedge into the risk-averse world of corporate book publishing. Our authors include Noam Chomsky, Arundhati Roy, Rebecca Solnit, Angela Davis, Howard Zinn, Amy Goodman, Wallace Shawn, Mike Davis, Winona LaDuke, Ilan Pappé, Richard Wolff, Dave Zirin, Keeanga-Yamahtta Taylor, Nick Turse, Dahr Jamail, David Barsamian, Elizabeth Laird, Amira Hass, Mark Steel, Avi Lewis, Naomi Klein, and Neil Davidson. We are also the trade publishers of the acclaimed Historical Materialism Book Series and of Dispatch Books.

also available from haymarket books

Before the Next Bomb Drops: Rising Up from Brooklyn to Palestine
Remi Kanazi

Black Girl Magic (forthcoming)
Edited by Mahogany Browne, Jamila Woods, and Idrissa Simmonds

The BreakBeat Poets: New American Poetry in the Age of Hip-Hop
Edited by Kevin Coval, Quraysh Ali Lansana, and Nate Marshall

Freedom Is a Constant Struggle: Ferguson, Palestine, and the Foundations of a Movement
Angela Y. Davis, edited by Frank Barat, preface by Cornel West

From #BlackLivesMatter to Black Liberation
Keeanga-Yamahtta Taylor

My Mother Was a Freedom Fighter
Aja Monet

A People's History of Chicago
Kevin Coval, Foreword by Chance the Rapper

Undivided Rights: Women of Color Organizing for Reproductive Justice
Jael Silliman, Marlene Gerber Fried, Loretta Ross, and Elena Gutiérrez